This book belongs to

Special Autographed Copy

. . . .

You are beautiful always!

Tony Moreland

Love who you are.

Jeanie Shor...

SEEK AND FIND

There are hidden hearts throughout the pages of this book.
As you seek the 43 hidden hearts, may it serve as a reminder of
Psalm 19:11. "Thy word have I hid in mine heart, that I might not sin against Thee." KJV

D1307211

Heart to Heart   *Publishing, Inc.*

Heart to Heart Publishing, Inc.
528 Mud Creek Road • Morgantown, KY 42261
(270) 526-5589
www.hearttoheartpublishinginc.com

Author: Tonya Moreland
Artist: Jeanie Shanks Kittinger
Senior editor: L.J. Gill
Editor: Patricia Craig
Designer: April Yingling- Jernigan

Printed in USA

First Edition
10 9 8 7 6 5 4 3 2

Heart to Heart Publishing, Inc. books are available at a special discount for bulk purchases in the US by corporations, institutions and other organizations. For more information, please contact Special Sales at 270-526-5589.

For Shelby and Sydney,
my precious gifts from God
Psalm 127:3 KJV

To bring glory to my Savior,
Jesus Christ
I Corinthians 10:31 KJV
-T.M.

Elizabeth Shanks Atcher who
has been my earthly rock,
and to God for his
unending generosity and
unconditional love.
-Jeanie

When Am I Beautiful?

Written by
Tonya Moreland

Illustrated by
Jeanie Shanks Kittinger

Daddy's little girl watched
as he gently kissed Mommy's
cheek and whispered,

"Have I told you you're **beautiful**
this morning?"

Mommy grinned bashfully.

With wonder on her face,
Daddy's little girl
raised her
eyes to meet her daddy's
and asked,

"Daddy, when am *I beautiful?*"

Daddy dropped to one knee,
gently placed her little hand in his
and said, "You are *beautiful* . . .

when you rise at dawn
with outstretched arms
and a great big yawn.

You are **beautiful** . . .

when you bake a cake
with flour in your hair
and icing on your face.

You are *beautiful* . . .

when your eyes are puffy
and your voice sounds funny
because your nose is stuffy.

You are *beautiful* . . .

with your lips bright red,
high heel shoes
and silly hats on your head.

You are *beautiful* . . .

when you make mud pies
with worms inside
for a big surprise.

You are *beautiful* . . .

when you wear fancy dresses,
all ready to go
with many colorful necklaces.

You are *beautiful* . . .

when you are wearing a smile
and even when you are
sad for a while.

You are *beautiful* . . .

when you splash in the tub
with your hair twirled up,
singing "Rub-a-Dub-Dub".

You are *beautiful* . . .

at night when stars fill the sky,
you lay your head down
and close your eyes.

You are **beautiful** now!

You see my little **beauty,**
God created you.
He chose the color of your hair and skin,
the color of your eyes,
and the shape of your nose and lips.
God designed you
and formed every part of you.
You are created in His image.

Do you understand what that means?"

"So God created man in his own image, in the image of God created he him; male and female created he them." Genesis 1:27 KJV
"For You formed my inward parts; You covered me in my mother's womb.[14] *I will praise You, for I am fearfully and wonderfully made; Marvelous are Your works, And that my soul knows very well."* Psalm 139: 13-14 KJV

Daddy's little girl stood tall, bright eyed,
and with a great big smile exclaimed,

"Of course, Daddy.
That means I am *beautiful ALWAYS,*
just like Mommy!"

Enjoy more learning activities and games to be used with *When Am I Beautiful?* at **www.tonya-moreland.com.**

Hidden Heart Answers:

Cover: 2 hearts (slippers)
Page 1: 5 hearts (mom's shirt, eggs)
Page 2: 2 hearts (kitchen cabinet)
Page 3: 2 hearts (dad's ear, little girl's sweater)
Page 4: 4 hearts (pillow, bear bow)
Page 5: 2 hearts (milk)
Page 6: 2 hearts (pillow, bed cover)
Page 7: 3 hearts (blue dress, bed skirt, hat)
Page 8: 4 heart (zipper, fence, tree, boot)
Page 9: 3 hearts (green dress, pink dress, play house)
Page 10: 4 hearts (background tree, fence)
Page 11: 2 hearts (vine, tree stump)
Page 12: 4 hearts (bear, bottom of page in black)
Page 13: 2 hearts (cabinet knobs)
Page 14: 2 hearts (cabinet knobs)